Original title:

Xeric Lights Beneath the Elf Pin

Copyright © 2025 Swan Charm

Author: Kene Elistrand

ISBN HARDBACK: 978-1-80562-720-3

ISBN PAPERBACK: 978-1-80564-241-1

Night's Wish Upon Thorny Petals

In twilight's hush, the shadows dance,
A wish upon a thorny glance.
Beneath the moon, where dreams ignite,
We gather starlit tales of night.

With every breath, the petals glow,
In gentle winds, soft secrets flow.
The whispers weave through leafy seams,
And hold the weight of broken dreams.

Where roses thorns do pierce the skin,
A truth profound, the heart locked in.
Yet in their grip, we find the strength,
To hope and heal, to go the length.

As night unfolds her velvet cloak,
The thorns speak softly, no harsh joke.
For every tear that falls like dew,
Finds solace in the love so true.

So cast your wish upon the breeze,
Among the thorns, beneath the trees.
For in the dark, where fears take flight,
Abides a spark, a glow of light.

Fables of Glowing Faery Whispers

In wooded glades where light does wane,
The faeries sing their sweet refrain.
With shimmering wings, they flit and play,
In twilight's arms, they find their way.

They whisper tales of olden days,
Of magic spun in sunlit rays.
In every turn, a fable grows,
In every heart, a secret glows.

From blooming chores in fragrant fields,
To silver streams where starlight yields.
Each glowing sprite, with laughter bright,
Joins in the dance of pure delight.

Their laughter echoes, soft and clear,
Bringing joy to hearts that hear.
For in their world, both wild and wide,
Alight the dreams that time can't hide.

So linger long in twilight's kiss,
And greet the dusk with gentle bliss.
For in each fable, whispered low,
A glimmering truth we come to know.

Light's Caress on Forgotten Roadways

Upon the trail where shadows blend,
A whisper of the light shall send.
Through cracks of earth and tangled vine,
The heart of day begins to shine.

With every step, the shadows sway,
As sunlight dances, bright and gay.
The whispers of the past entwined,
In golden threads that fate has lined.

Embers glow in twilight's breath,
The pathway sings of life and death.
Yet in this realm where dreams take flight,
The light will guide us through the night.

So let your fears be swept away,
Embrace the dawn of this new day.
For on these roads, lost yet found,
The whispers of the light abound.

And as we journey through the haze,
The warmth of hope forever stays.
Through every bend and turn we tread,
We'll find our way where dreams are led.

Aetherial Dawn in Silent Valleys

In valleys hushed where echoes fade,
The morning breaks, a golden blade.
Aetherial light, so soft and sweet,
Caressing earth with gentle feet.

With every sigh, the shadows part,
Revealing beauty in nature's heart.
The whispers of the night retreat,
As colors merge in daylight's greet.

The moth and bloom in quiet dance,
In swirling light, they take a chance.
To paint the air with colors bright,
In silent valleys, hearts alight.

The breath of dawn, a tender kiss,
Unlocks the world's forgotten bliss.
As dreams awaken, still and free,
In every soul, the light shall be.

And as we wander hand in hand,
Through valleys vast, on golden sand,
The aether's glow will guide our way,
In silent whispers of the day.

Secrets Bound in Celestial Embrace

Beneath the night, the stars unfold,
Their secrets bright, in stories told.
In whispers soft, the heavens sigh,
A cosmic dance, where dreams can fly.

Each twinkling light a tale unspooled,
In secrets that the night has ruled.
With every gaze, we seek to find,
The truths that linger, unconfined.

In shadows deep, where echoes dwell,
The universe weaves its silent spell.
With every heart that dares to dream,
A spark ignites, a radiant beam.

The cosmos breathes, a lullaby,
To cradle hopes and let them fly.
In celestial arms, we find our peace,
As whispered secrets never cease.

So let the stars illuminate the night,
With cosmic guidance, pure and bright.
For in their glow, the heart takes flight,
In secrets bound, we find our light.

Dreamweaver's Light Amongst the Ruins

Within the ruins, shadows cast,
A dreamweaver's light, a spell so vast.
Among the stones where time has worn,
New visions rise, rebirth is born.

Each fractured wall, a tale to tell,
Of lives once lived, where hearts would swell.
The dreamer's spark ignites the past,
In every whisper, magic's cast.

Through crumbling arches, dreams take shape,
In every crack, anew escape.
The light shall weave a tapestry,
Of hopes renewed in memory.

With every step through ancient halls,
The dreamweaver's smile gently calls.
To stitch the tales that time ignored,
In every silence, the light restored.

So wander here, where echoes play,
And let the light guide every sway.
In ruins deep, where dreams ignite,
The dreamweaver's light, our endless night.

Whimsical Lights in the Dry Afternoon

In the stillness of the sun,
A dance of shadows has begun.
Golden rays on barren land,
Whimsical lights, a soft command.

Cacti sway with gentle grace,
A fleeting smile on nature's face.
With every breeze, the whispers call,
The afternoon beckons, a magic thrall.

Colors burst, a painter's dream,
Rivulets of light that gleam.
In laughter, children chase the breeze,
Underneath the swaying trees.

Like memories of a distant song,
Beneath the heat, they hum along.
Each flicker tells a tale anew,
In a world that's vivid and true.

As twilight nears, the lights will fade,
A soft farewell that spirits laid.
Yet in our hearts, they linger still,
Whimsical hopes that time can't kill.

Whispers of the Dune Oasis

Amid the dunes, a secret sigh,
In shadows deep where whispers lie.
The palm trees bow to the soft breeze,
As sunbeams dance with grace and ease.

Rippling waters, a mirage bright,
Calling wanderers in the night.
A hidden gem in golden sand,
Where dreams are formed by nature's hand.

Laughter mingles with the flow,
Stories shared in the afterglow.
Beneath the stars, the spirits rise,
Where every glance brings wistful sighs.

The moon whispers tales of old,
As heartbeats echo, brave and bold.
In this haven, all is peace,
As gentle winds grant sweet release.

The oasis blooms with scents divine,
Under the watch of a starlit vine.
Embrace the magic held so close,
In whispers soft, we find our prose.

Ethereal Glow in Thistle Shade

In thistle shade, a glow appears,
A soft embrace that calms our fears.
Beneath the boughs, where secrets dwell,
The light weaves stories only time can tell.

Petals blush in violet hue,
While beams of sunlight pierce right through.
The air is thick with fragrant dreams,
As nature hums in soft moonbeams.

With every rustle, a whisper shared,
A tapestry of love declared.
In shadow's arms, we're bound and free,
Enchanted by this tapestry.

Here, the spirit finds its song,
In the stillness where we belong.
With every moment, magic grows,
In thistle shade, our wonder flows.

As twilight paints the world in gold,
Each heartbeat thrums with tales untold.
Ethereal glow, a gentle friend,
In this hushed realm where dreams transcend.

Enchanted Nocturne of the Desert

Beneath a canvas rich and dark,
The desert hums a midnight spark.
With constellations, stories twine,
In every star, a glance divine.

The sands, they sing a melody,
Of ancient times, of destiny.
As moonlight bathes the world in white,
An enchanted tale unfolds at night.

Cacti loom like sentinels bold,
Guardians of secrets, stories told.
Whispers travel on the breeze,
Carrying dreams through midnight trees.

With every shadow, more unfolds,
A touch of magic, brave and bold.
The night is alive, a rich delight,
In the heart of the desert, purest light.

As dawn approaches, colors blend,
A promise kept, a journey's end.
Yet in our hearts, the magic stays,
An enchanted nocturne, forever plays.

Threads of Light in the Barren Vale

In the vale where shadows creep,
Whispers of old secrets seep.
Threads of gold in twilight weave,
And hearts find magic to believe.

A breeze like laughter fills the air,
As stars begin their gentle flare.
Each glimmer holds a tale untold,
Of dreams and futures bright and bold.

With every step on ancient stone,
Echoes of the past are sown.
The silence hums a forgotten song,
A rhythm that has lingered long.

Amidst the thorns, the flowers bloom,
Chasing away the lingering gloom.
In this place where hopes ignite,
Threads of light make darkness bright.

Elfin Dreams Amidst the Sundrenched Canopy

Beneath the leaves where sunlight streams,
The air is thick with elfin dreams.
Sylvan whispers softly call,
Inviting all to heed their thrall.

In every branch a story hides,
Where magic stirs and time abides.
The playful fays on breezes glide,
While moonlit shadows stretch and bide.

A crystal brook sings sweet and clear,
With laughter dancing in its cheer.
Beneath the boughs, the dreams unfold,
As secrets in the silence hold.

Golden rays through emerald lace,
Transform the woods into a grace.
In every glade, enchantments rise,
Elfin worlds beneath wide skies.

Flickering Enchantment on the Gnarled Roots

Down by the river, old and wide,
Gnarled roots twist, in shadows hide.
Flickering lights like fireflies play,
Guiding the lost who've gone astray.

In the hush of the evening's glow,
Whispers of magic, soft and slow.
A tapestry of ancient night,
Woven with dreams, both dark and bright.

The air is thick with olden lore,
Echoes of times that came before.
Each flicker dances, tales to share,
Of spirits hidden, everywhere.

Through tangled vines, the wonders grow,
Where only the brave dare to go.
Hold onto hope, for it's the key,
To unlock the roots of mystery.

Shadows Dance in the Moon's Caress

When the silver moon begins to rise,
Shadows dance beneath the skies.
Whirling and twirling, soft and free,
In the quiet night, they find their spree.

Among the trees, they weave and sway,
In a luminous, spectral ballet.
Each whisper cradles the dreams of night,
In silken veils of pale moonlight.

The silver beams kiss the earth below,
As starlit secrets begin to flow.
In the hush, a symphony swells,
Drawing forth forgotten spells.

Together they swirl, shadows and light,
Creating magic in the night.
A dance so sweet beneath the skies,
Where time stands still and wonder lies.

LLumined Paths of Dry Desires

In shadowed corners of the day,
A whisper calls to hearts astray.
With every step on weary ground,
Lost dreams and hopes begin to sound.

The air is thick with dusky light,
Yet sparks of wishful thoughts ignite.
A path once forged in muted stone,
Now shimmers bright, as if it's known.

Beneath the weight of barren skies,
The echoes dance, the spirit flies.
With careful tread, the seeker roams,
To find the place where longing homes.

And through the dust of time's embrace,
A fleeting glimpse of truth and grace.
What once was lost comes into view,
As fires of desire burn anew.

In Llumined paths, a journey starts,
With every twist, they guard their hearts.
Through dry desires, they boldly stride,
With hope aligned, they choose their guide.

Starlight Reflections on Forgotten Trails

The stars, they weave a silver song,
Guiding souls who've wandered long.
With every twinkle, tales unfold,
Of journeys past, of brave and bold.

The forgotten trails, they whisper low,
Where secrets dwell and shadows grow.
Each step recalls a distant dream,
Unraveling threads of life's grand scheme.

In night's embrace, the heartbeats blend,
With echoes of a time unpenned.
Reflections caught in starlit streams,
Awake the slumbering, ancient themes.

And in the calm of moonlit nights,
The wanderer seeks what feels just right.
In every gleam, a promise glows,
Of paths reborn and love that flows.

Through starlit reflections, fate shall weave,
In forgotten tales, the heart believes.
Each journey taken leads anew,
In cosmic dances, life's rich view.

Beacons of the Hidden Glade

In cloistered woods where whispers cease,
The beacons shine, a call for peace.
Amidst the trees, where shadows dwell,
A hidden glade, a mystic spell.

With gentle light, the lanterns soar,
Illuminating paths of yore.
Where every leaf and blade of grass,
Reflects the stories, long since passed.

The fragrance of the earth entwined,
Revealing secrets nature's mined.
A symphony of rustling leaves,
Wraps every heart as it believes.

Within the glade, the spirits dance,
In flickering light, a fleeting chance.
To touch the magic, feel the grace,
Of ancient lore in this safe space.

Beacons guiding through the trees,
Their glow inspires, invites to seize.
In hidden glades, the world can see,
The beauty bound in harmony.

Evening Songs of the Sagebrush Spirits

As twilight drapes the desert wide,
The sagebrush stirs, the spirits bide.
With evening songs, they softly hum,
A melody where dreams are spun.

In the golden hues of fading light,
The whispering winds, a gentle rite.
Each note a tale of ages past,
Of love and loss, forever cast.

The spirits rise with the setting sun,
In every echo, a journey begun.
Through dusty trails, their voices weave,
In every heart, a chance to believe.

The canvas changes, colors blend,
As evening's charms descend, transcend.
With every breath, the night ignites,
As sagebrush spirits grace the nights.

Their songs remind of paths untread,
Of dreams that linger, words unsaid.
In evening's glow, the soul takes flight,
Embracing all the magic of night.

Luminous Secrets of the Faery Grove

In the grove where whispers throng,
Tiny lights in the dusk do sing.
A tapestry of dreams so strong,
Underneath the silver-wing.

Dancing shadows weave the night,
A secret kept by the ancient trees.
Glow of magic, soft and bright,
Fluttering like a gentle breeze.

Mossy carpets softly hum,
To the tune of faery delight.
In this realm, the heartbeats drum,
Beneath the pale moon's light.

Where wishes blend with starlit mist,
The paths are marked with dreams untold.
Each flicker is a parting gift,
Of tales from a world so bold.

In each corner, treasures lie,
Waiting for the brave to find.
As the night begins to sigh,
The secrets leave the earth confined.

Shadows Cast by Starlit Cacti

In the desert's vast embrace,
Cacti stand like silent guards.
Beneath the stars, their shadows race,
Painting stories on the shards.

Moonlight kisses every thorn,
Guided by the night-bird's call.
Whispers float like dreams reborn,
Casting spells that lift and fall.

Glimmers dance on sand's dark sea,
In the stillness, time does pause.
Cacti bloom so brilliantly,
Against the night, they form a cause.

Echoes of the past resound,
In the hush, a soft refrain.
With each star, a tale is found,
Of love, of loss, and of the pain.

Here in shadows, mysteries play,
As the night unfolds its map.
Follow where the stories sway,
Underneath the starlit cap.

Dreamscapes in the Arid Night

Underneath the wide expanse,
Night unveils its secret net.
Stars begin their silent dance,
Where dreams and tender hopes are set.

Cacti sigh beneath the moon,
Each breath a flicker of the past.
Whispers rise like sweet perfume,
In the still, the die is cast.

Every grain of sand imbues,
A memory lost to time's embrace.
As shadows blend, the heart renews,
In the endless, starry space.

With each twinkle, dreams ignite,
Filling hearts with hope anew.
The desert sings its lullabies,
In this vast, enchanted view.

Come and tread the dreamy path,
Where whispers guide the weary soul.
In arid night, find love's sweet hearth,
Where gentle shadows play their role.

Glimmers of the Elven Mirage

Where the rivers weave and flow,
Elfin lights softly gleam.
In the twilight, secrets show,
Crafting every whispered dream.

Mirages dance on twilight's loom,
Casting spells of fleeting grace.
Amidst the trees, an ancient bloom,
Hides the silence of their place.

In the glen where shadows twine,
Songs of ages past arise.
Each glimmer, a fading sign,
Awakening the night's disguise.

Lost within this magic realm,
Where spirits play in laughter bright.
In elven mist, we find the helm,
To guide us through the extended night.

Join the dance, let heartstrings flow,
In the echoes of the past.
The elven mirage will bestow,
A tale of peace that loves to last.

Glowing Visions of the Enchanted Vale

In the vale where whispers rue,
Softly echoes grace anew.
Misty mornings, visions bright,
Dancing beams of morning light.

Ancient trees, their branches weave,
Tales of old, the heart believes.
In shadows where the secrets lay,
Magic breathes in soft array.

Crystal streams with laughter spill,
Carrying dreams, a tranquil thrill.
Flowers bloom with colors pure,
Enchanting hearts, a sweet allure.

Through the fog, the spirits glide,
Guiding souls with gentle pride.
In this vale, where magic swells,
Live the stories that it tells.

So close your eyes, and you may see,
Wonders born from fantasy.
In the vale of joy and grace,
Life's true magic finds its place.

Flickering Gems of the Great Expanse

Stars like jewels in midnight's crown,
Whispers across the sky renown.
Winds unveil the lore they hold,
Flickering tales of the bold.

Through vast skies, the secrets lie,
Woven deep and soaring high.
Constellations paint the night,
Gems of glory, pure delight.

Echoes of the ancient fire,
In their glow, we find desire.
Navigators, hearts aflame,
Searching for the lost, the same.

Across the fields where shadows play,
Dreamers chase the night away.
Flickering hopes dance in our veins,
The cosmos sings, its name remains.

So lift your eyes, embrace the vast,
In the gems, the die is cast.
For every star, a story told,
In the expanse, our dreams unfold.

Glow of the Forgotten Nymphs

In the glen where whispers sigh,
Forgotten nymphs weave by.
Echoes of their laughter sweet,
In gentle rills, their hearts repeat.

Mossy stones, a secret throne,
Guard the tales of dreams long flown.
Glimmers fade, yet still they play,
In twilight's gleam, they find their way.

Each flicker sparks a hidden grace,
In the shadows, they find space.
Like a breeze through willow's sigh,
They twirl beneath the twilight sky.

Moonlit paths of dreams unspooled,
In the night, their magic ruled.
Forgotten yet, they softly call,
To hearts who heed their silent thrall.

So listen close, for in the night,
Their stories pulse with pure delight.
Nymphs of old, forever dwell,
In the glow of the forest spell.

Nightfall Beyond the Thorns

As shadows stretch and daylight wanes,
Nightfall cloaks the whispered plains.
Beneath the thorns, a silence weaves,
Where secrets dwell and hope believes.

In twilight's glow, the stars ignite,
Painting dreams with silver light.
Thorny paths may twist and wind,
But through the darkness, joy we find.

Lurking fears take flight once more,
Yet courage knocks upon the door.
With every heartbeat, truth unfolds,
In moonlit tales, our fate beholds.

So journey forth, embrace the night,
For in the dark, our spirits fight.
Beyond the thorns, a promise waits,
To weave our dreams with opened gates.

In every shadow, light shall gleam,
Flickering softly, hope's sweet dream.
So venture forth, brave hearts, be drawn,
To the dawn that comes with every morn.

Starlit Crypts of the Dryland

In the hush of the evening's grasp,
Whispers echo through time's smooth past.
Beneath the stars, the secrets sleep,
In crypts where shadows gently creep.

Velvet skies with a twinkling face,
Guarding truths in their velvet space.
Each star a story, a wish unspun,
In the dryland's heart, where dreams have run.

Footsteps linger on shifting sands,
Carried forth by unseen hands.
A ghostly dance of fluttering light,
Guides the lost through the veil of night.

From silence deep, a song will rise,
Beneath the wide and watchful skies.
With every breath, they weave and twine,
In starlit crypts where spirits shine.

So linger long, in magic's grasp,
And in the dark, let your heart clasp.
For in these spaces, so wide and vast,
The dryland's dreams forever last.

Vine of Illumination from Cavernous Dreams

In the depths where shadows glide,
A vine of light does softly hide.
It winds through tales of yesteryear,
Illuminating paths we hold dear.

Glimmers glow in the eerie gloom,
Whispers of hope from the cavern's womb.
Each tendril reaches, each leaf is spun,
A dance of hopes 'neath the silvered sun.

Tangled threads of fate entwine,
In this realm where wishes shine.
With every pulse, the magic grows,
The vine of dreams in twilight flows.

Time stands still as stories weave,
In cavernous depths, we dare believe.
Threads of memory softly gleam,
A tapestry crafted from a dream.

So touch the vine and feel the spark,
In the shadows, find your mark.
With every heartbeat, the truths will spark,
From the cavern's heart, a light in the dark.

Ethereal Sands of Memory and Light

Across the dunes where shadows hum,
Ethereal sands in whispers come.
Each grain a moment, a flickered glance,
In the tapestry of fate's great dance.

Time drifts lightly on breezes fair,
Painting stories with tender care.
Reflections shimmer in sun's warm glow,
As memories rise like the tides that flow.

Veils of mist in the golden dawn,
Wrap the secrets of dreams long gone.
Soft echoes meld with the desert's sigh,
Beneath the vast and endless sky.

With every step on the shifting ground,
The whispers of ages can still be found.
In ethereal sands, where heartbeats dwell,
The tales of hope and loss we tell.

So breathe in deep, let the moments blend,
In the dance of light where shadows mend.
For the sands of time are forever bright,
In the heart of memory and light.

Nightfall's Glistening Breath

As twilight cloaks the world in shade,
Nightfall's breath begins to invade.
With every whisper, the stars ignite,
Casting glistening dreams through the night.

A symphony stirs in the velvet air,
Softly wrapping the earth with care.
Each flicker of light, a promise spun,
In the dance of the moon, the new day begun.

Beneath the canopy, shadows play,
Chasing away the remnants of day.
Mysteries rise with the misty glee,
Unraveling tales of what's yet to be.

So listen closely, the night recalls,
The lullabies sung through ancient halls.
With every sigh, the magic's found,
In the glistening breath that swathes the ground.

Embrace the darkness, let fears take flight,
For nightfall's glisten is pure delight.
With every moment, a door swings wide,
To the realm where dreams and shadows collide.

Aurora of the Elusive Grove

In whispers soft the dawn awaits,
Where shadows dance with gentle fates,
A tapestry of glimmered dreams,
Where magic flows in silver streams.

Among the trees, a eldritch light,
That beckons forth the brave of sight,
It shimmers on each leafed embrace,
As secrets bloom in hidden space.

The winds of fate through branches weave,
A symphony that few believe,
Yet here the heart finds gentle rest,
Wrapped in the warmth of nature's best.

Each step a note, each breath a rhyme,
In harmony, we halt in time,
Bonded by earth and sky's soft song,
In this enchanted grove, we belong.

So wander deep, let wonder guide,
Through every shadow, every tide,
For in this grove, the world transforms,
As dawn awakens magic's storms.

Beacons Among the Barren Branches

In twilight's grasp, when shadows creep,
A flicker stirs from slumber deep,
These beacons shine through barren space,
With glimmers sweet, they light the place.

A glint of hope on rugged bark,
Unveils the path through mist and dark,
Each starlet whispers tales of old,
Of love and valor, brave and bold.

Through windswept branches, flickers turn,
As hearts entwine and lanterns burn,
In solitude, they softly gleam,
Each ember holds a wistful dream.

With every pulse, the night expands,
Golden lights like guiding hands,
Among the roots where stories dwell,
In quietude, we weave our spell.

Oh, wondrous woods, so wild yet tame,
In your embrace, we cast our name,
From barren limbs, our spirits rise,
Like beacons bright among the skies.

Ethereal Flickers in Nature's Tapestry

Upon the leaves, a shimmer glows,
A dance of light where magic flows,
With every flicker, tales unfold,
In whispered hush, their truths are told.

The colors swirl in vibrant hues,
Crafted by nature's gentle muse,
Each thread a wish, each knot a dream,
In this rich tapestry, we scheme.

Through dappled shade and sun-kissed ground,
Where every heartbeat echoes sound,
A symphony of life awake,
In every breath, our spirits shake.

With every gust, the stories weave,
In every sigh, they dance, believe,
The flickers flutter, soft and bright,
Creating worlds in dark and light.

So let us wander, hand in hand,
Through timeless fields, where dreams expand,
For in this realm of soft delight,
Ethereal flickers guide our flight.

Lost in the Glow of Nature's Heart

In twilight's arms, we find our place,
A warm embrace, a gentle grace,
Where every leaf and petal sighs,
And starlit dreams fill up the skies.

With every step, the wilds display,
An artful path, where shadows play,
Among the blooms, a fragrant trail,
In nature's choir, we join the tale.

The glow of dusk, a soft caress,
In nature's heart, we are blessed,
In every rustle, every breeze,
The whispered secrets bring us ease.

So linger long where magic dwells,
In quiet corners, stories swell,
For in this glow, our spirits soar,
Forever lost, forever more.

Beneath the stars, as night enfolds,
The heart of nature softly holds,
In golden light, we find our way,
In harmony, we wish to stay.

Glimmers in Arid Shadows

In the twilight's gentle grip,
The shadows softly play,
Glimmers dance on thirsty sand,
As night begins its sway.

A coyote's haunting call,
Echoes through the vale,
Stars emerge as silent guards,
In this desert tale.

Each breeze a whispered secret,
Among the ancient bones,
Time stands still in golden hues,
Where silence softly moans.

The moonlight paints the earth,
In shimmering silver dreams,
A world alive with magic,
Or so it surely seems.

Beneath the vast, eternal sky,
Hope flickers like a flame,
In the heart of arid shadows,
Nothing ever stays the same.

Whispers of the Dryland Canopy

Beneath the eaves of withered trees,
Where secrets twist and tangle,
Whispers drift like autumn leaves,
In a soft and gentle jangle.

The sun's embrace grows faint and frail,
As dusk descends with grace,
Creatures stir in quietude,
In their hidden, sacred place.

The branches weave a timeless tale,
In patterns old and wise,
Of dreams that bathe the dryland,
Underneath the vast, blue skies.

Rustling leaves share stories told,
Of journeys vast and wide,
Of wanderers who sought the light,
Through the shadows they did slide.

So linger in the twilight,
Let the dryland speak its truth,
For every whisper bears a thread,
Of wisdom in our youth.

Starlit Secrets of the Forbidden Grove

In the heart of the night, a grove does bloom,
With secrets wrapped in silver light,
Each star a watchful keeper,
Of dreams that take their flight.

Hidden paths of ancient stone,
Weave through the tangled trees,
Where shadows meet in quiet dance,
And spirits drift with ease.

A breeze, a sigh, a whispered name,
In the air, a sweet perfume,
The stories of the lost unfold,
In this enchanted room.

Moonbeams cast a gentle glow,
On petals soft and bright,
Within the depths of the forbidden,
Magic kisses the night.

So follow where the starlight leads,
Into the grove's embrace,
For every heart that dares to dream,
Finds their rightful place.

Dancing Flames of the Desert Night

Underneath the midnight sky,
Where shadows stretch and sway,
Dancing flames of flickering light,
Cast warmth upon the clay.

Embers whisper tales of old,
Of wanderers on their quest,
Each flicker tells a story,
Of trials and of rest.

The desert blooms in fiery hues,
As stars begin to cheer,
In this moment, wild and free,
All sorrows disappear.

Around the fire, voices rise,
In harmony and song,
The flames twist like a serenade,
Where every heart belongs.

So let the night embrace your soul,
As the desert sings its tune,
In dancing flames of magic,
We find our light, our moon.

The Forgotten Glow of the Enchanted Glade

In shadows deep where whispers dwell,
The ancient trees weave magic's spell.
With roots like veins, the secrets spread,
A tapestry of dreams long fled.

The moonlight dances on silver streams,
A flickering light in silent dreams.
Remembered tales of faery kin,
In every leaf, their laughter's din.

The glow arises from mossy beds,
Where time's embrace gently treads.
Each petal soft, each breeze a song,
Invites the heart to linger long.

With every step the spirits sigh,
In echoing woods where secrets lie.
A glade of wonder, cloaked in night,
Still whispers warmth, still holds the light.

At Dawn's Edge, a Hidden Flame

As dawn breaks soft on golden fields,
A whispered hush the daylight yields.
The dew like jewels on blades of grass,
Glimmers sweetly as shadows pass.

Birds break the silence with songs so clear,
Heralds of hope that draw so near.
In the heart of morn, where dreams converge,
A hidden blaze begins to surge.

The sun spills gold on the waking world,
In tender light, new stories unfurled.
Each ray a thread in the tapestry bright,
Weaving wonders into the night.

Where once was doubt, now courage stands,
With open hearts and willing hands.
At dawn's soft edge, life starts to climb,
Unlocking valleys lost to time.

Nocturnal Glimmers in Dusk's Embrace

When twilight settles, deep and slow,
The stars awake, a gentle glow.
In quiet corners where shadows play,
Secrets linger of the day.

The trees stand tall, their leaves a-sway,
Guardians of night, they softly sway.
The hush of dusk is laced with dreams,
An echoing pulse of night's sweet schemes.

Moonbeams dance upon the lake,
Each ripple sings of promises to make.
In sacred stillness, hearts align,
Beneath the stars, we learn to shine.

In every glimmer, hope remains,
A spark of light that never wanes.
As night enfolds, we weave our fate,
In twilight's arms, we contemplate.

Radiant Visions Amongst the Crumbling Bark

In forests deep where whispers dwell,
Amidst the vines, a tale to tell.
The ancient trees, with wisdom vast,
Stand sentinel to memories cast.

Beneath the boughs, where shadows lie,
Radiant visions begin to fly.
In cracks of bark, the glories shine,
With every twist, a story divine.

The sunlight pierces through the leaves,
Crafting patterns each heart believes.
In every crevice, in every hue,
The echoes of magic come rushing through.

As time unwinds and seasons change,
The haunting beauty seems so strange.
Yet still it breathes in the echo's mark,
In crumbling bark, we find the spark.

Whispering Captivities of the Glinting Spires

Amidst the towers, secrets glide,
A song of echoes, shadows hide.
The wind weaves tales of yore,
In whispers soft, they ever soar.

Glistening points reach for the sky,
While dreams in silence dare to fly.
In twilight's grasp, the night unfolds,
A tapestry of stories told.

With every spark that flickers bright,
A hint of magic in the night.
The heart of stone begins to thrum,
As gentle voices beckon, come.

In moonlit glades where spirits dwell,
The spires hold their secret spell.
Bound in dreams, the lost remain,
In glinting hues, they birth their gain.

So heed the calls of soaring heights,
Within the spires, lives pure delights.
The whispering winds, forever sing,
Of glinting glories, time shall bring.

Intrigues of the Starlit Arroyos

Beneath the stars, the waters gleam,
Carving tales through a midnight dream.
In shadows where the soft streams flow,
Whispers of secrets gently grow.

Flickering lights dance in the dark,
As mysteries unfold with a spark.
The arroyos weave their silent lore,
A tapestry of moments, evermore.

Through ancient paths where whispers trace,
The echoes of forgotten grace.
With every twist, a tale is spun,
In harmony with night and sun.

Beneath the arches of a silver sky,
In murmurs soft, the spirits fly.
Their laughter joins the bubbling stream,
In starlit veins, they weave a dream.

So follow where the water leads,
In starlit arroyos, heart proceeds.
Adventure waits in every bend,
As intrigue dances without end.

Glowing Chronicles of the Wandering Shadows

In twilight's glow, the shadows roam,
Painting tales of a distant home.
Secrets cloaked in midnight's hue,
Chronicles old, yet thrillingly new.

They glide through trees, both tall and wise,
Reflecting dreams beneath the skies.
With each soft step, the stories blend,
A whispered thread that has no end.

Beneath the stars, forgotten lore,
In shadowed realms, the heart will soar.
Fragments of time in dance unite,
Illuminated by the moon's bright light.

Wandering spirits, lost and found,
In glowing paths, their voices sound.
From every corner, echoes rise,
In shimmering glints that mesmerize.

So tread the lines where shadows play,
In glowing tales that softly sway.
Each step you take, a tale you weave,
In wandering shadows, dare to believe.

Phantoms of Radiant Paths

A lightened trail where phantoms tread,
In whispered truths, they gently said.
Each step reveals a story bright,
On radiant paths, a gilded light.

With every footfall, echoes dance,
In spectral realms, souls find their chance.
The woven threads of fate entwine,
In shimmering moments that align.

Through fields of gold and skies of blue,
The phantoms roam, both wise and true.
In glistening dawns, they find their way,
Through radiant paths, forever stay.

A symphony of sighs and dreams,
In every corner, laughter beams.
Within the light, they gently sway,
Enchanting hearts, come what may.

So follow where the phantoms guide,
In radiant paths, let spirit ride.
For every turn holds magic's breath,
In glowing trails that cheat the death.

Elysian Lightfall Through Thorny Arches

In twilight gleam, the shadows weave,
Through thorny paths, where dreams believe.
A whisper calls, upon the night,
As stars emerge, in soft delight.

Among the boughs, the fae do glide,
With laughter light, where secrets hide.
They twirl and spin, in moonlit dance,
Beneath the gaze of fate's romance.

The arches bloom, with petals rare,
In fragrant air, of sweet despair.
The heavens drip, with silver dew,
A tapestry of colors new.

Each flitting heart, a songbird's grace,
In Elysium's warm embrace.
While candlelight in silence hums,
With every breath, a magic comes.

Pathways glow, where spirits tread,
Through thorns of dreams, and hopes long shed.
The light cascades, like morning mist,
In every moment, not to be missed.

Dance of the Ethereal Blossoms

In gardens vast, the blossoms sway,
With gentle poise in bright array.
Their colors sing, a soft refrain,
While breezes whisper through the lane.

The moonlit glow, in silver streams,
Awakens night with fragrant dreams.
The petals twirl, in chanted light,
A ballet spun of pure delight.

In shadows deep, where secrets bloom,
Each flower's grace dispels the gloom.
The stars align, a wondrous sight,
As blossoms dance in soft twilight.

With every step, the cosmos sighs,
As gentle laughter fills the skies.
An ethereal waltz, the night bestows,
In whispered vows, the magic grows.

They sway and twirl, in moonlit air,
In perfect harmony, beyond compare.
A dance of dreams, with hearts entwined,
In nature's arms, true peace we find.

Luring Glimmers in the Ductile Night

In dusky realms where shadows crawl,
A flicker hints, a whispered call.
The night unfolds, with glimmers bright,
That lure us forth, into the light.

Within the dark, the secrets play,
As fleeting phantoms drift away.
With every twinkle, hope ignites,
A dance of fate in ductile nights.

Through silvered fields of starlit dreams,
The world around us softly gleams.
Each radiant spark, a tale to tell,
In moonlit realms where wonders dwell.

A beckoning glow, on paths of grace,
With magic woven, in time and space.
The night enfolds, as spirits rise,
In luminescence, shadows die.

We wander forth, the path obscured,
By glimmers bright, in joy secured.
With every step, the heart takes flight,
In luring glimmers of the night.

Secrets Enshrined in Moonlit Shadows

Beneath the glow of silver beams,
Are hidden truths in whispered dreams.
In twilight's arms, where phantoms play,
Secrets enshrined, kept at bay.

The forest breathes, a melody,
In shadows deep, where none can see.
The owls of night, they guard the lore,
Of ancient tales, forevermore.

Through winding paths, the stories flow,
Of lovers lost, and hearts aglow.
In moonlit threnodies they sing,
Of fleeting time and everything.

Every rustle, a promise speaks,
The essence of the night's mystique.
Where echoes linger, softly rise,
In moonlit shadows, love never dies.

So heed the call of whispered sighs,
And let your heart, like eagle, rise.
For in the night, when all is still,
The veils of time, we dare to thrill.

Moonlit Dancer in Sagebrush

In the hush of night, she twirls,
Woven dreams in tender swirls.
Stars above, a silvery light,
Guiding steps through endless night.

Whispers weave through thorny beds,
Secrets dance in twilight threads.
Sagebrush rustles, soft and low,
Nature's rhythm, sweet and slow.

Her laughter mingles with the breeze,
Carried forth through ancient trees.
Each twinkling star a watchful eye,
As the moon paints paths in the sky.

A fleeting shadow, a silent trace,
Embracing the night in a warm embrace.
With every leap, the world stands still,
Captured moments, a heart to fill.

In the dusk where dreams ignite,
The dancer weaves through twinkling light.
With each step, a story unfolds,
Of moonlit nights and whispered holds.

Celestial Flickers on Dried Earth

Beneath the heavens, a symphony plays,
Echoes of twilight in dusky haze.
Flickers of stars on parched terrain,
Whispers of magic in the soft rain.

Each speck of dust catching glimmers bright,
Stories woven from the depths of night.
The air hums softly, secrets to share,
As cosmic wonders linger in the air.

With each gentle breeze, tales take flight,
Every heartbeat a spark of light.
The ground beneath, cracked and worn,
Yet still it cradles, a promise reborn.

Time stretches thin in the space between,
Where dreams dance lightly, never unseen.
Celestial sparks ignite the dark,
Guiding us gently with each fleeting mark.

From dried earth come the echoes of old,
Dreams forged anew, tales yet untold.
In this magic, we quietly bask,
As the stars listen, enshrined in their task.

Mysteries of the Dusk Bloom

When the day surrenders to the night,
Colors fade, but ghosts take flight.
In the shadows, secrets thrive,
The dusk blooms softly, hopes arrive.

Petals whisper of dreams untold,
In twilight's embrace, the night turns gold.
Fragrant scents on the evening air,
Draw us closer, the heart laid bare.

Each moment twirls in a gentle race,
Dusk reveals its tender grace.
A silent witness, the creeping night,
Gathering stories to share with light.

With tangled roots and shadows deep,
The mysteries beckon, enticing sleep.
In every corner, magic lays,
Waiting to be found in playful ways.

As the moon climbs high, a silver thread,
It weaves through slumber, gently spread.
The dusk blooms vibrant, night sings true,
In its embrace, we find anew.

Radiant Echoes of the Sand

In the desert's heart, where silence reigns,
Echoes of wanderers weave through the plains.
Grains of sand catch the sun's last glaze,
Whispers of timeless, forgotten ways.

Footprints carved in the golden hue,
Each step a story, each story true.
Beneath the stars, where shadows meld,
Radiant secrets of the earth upheld.

With every breeze, the dunes shift slow,
Carrying tales from long ago.
A language spoken in rustling tones,
Binding together the ancient stones.

Amidst the stillness, a fire ignites,
Passion and longing in star-kissed nights.
Fleeting moments in the sands cascade,
Echoes of dreams that never fade.

In twilight's glow, the world stands bright,
The desert whispers to the night.
Radiant echoes call us near,
In the heart of sand, we lose our fear.

Enchanted Beams Amongst the Sagebrush

In a land where shadows dance at dusk,
Sagebrush sways with secrets hushed.
Moonlight spills on golden sands,
A whisper from the ancient lands.

Stars peek through the twilight veil,
Casting spells where dreamers sail.
Each breeze a song, soft and sweet,
Guiding hearts where wonders meet.

Timid flowers bloom with grace,
In this enchanted, hidden space.
Night unfolds its tapestry,
As magic drifts, so wild and free.

Underneath the purple sky,
The echoes of the night birds fly.
Gentle murmurs ride the air,
Nature weaves a charm so rare.

With each stride through silvery dew,
Promises of dreams come true.
The sagebrush sways, the night ignites,
In the arms of starry nights.

Echoes of Luminous Lullabies

In the quiet of the evening glow,
Soft echoes of lullabies flow.
Moonbeams dance on glimmering streams,
Swaying gently with twilight dreams.

A serenade from the sleeping trees,
Carried lightly by the breeze.
Crickets weave their nightly song,
In this world where hearts belong.

Stars blink in a cosmic choir,
Stirring souls with gentle fire.
Whispers wrap the world in peace,
In the night's embrace, worries cease.

Each note a tale of love and light,
Beneath the fabric of the night.
A symphony of dreams untold,
In harmony with hearts so bold.

As dreams take flight on silver wings,
Echoes of hope and joy it brings.
Luminous tales from above,
In every heart, there blooms the love.

Celestial Whispers in a Parched Land

A barren stretch beneath the sun,
Where day meets night, the shadows run.
Through cracked earth and silent sighs,
Hope blossoms where the spirit lies.

In the stillness, a soft breeze calls,
Dancing lightly 'midst dusty walls.
Celestial whispers fill the air,
Reminding all that dreams still dare.

Stars twinkle like diamonds rare,
Painting wishes on the air.
Each twinkling light a tale it tells,
Of magic found in barren spells.

The moon's embrace, a soothing balm,
Restores the land with soothing calm.
As shadows blend with vibrant hues,
The heart awakens, and hope renews.

In this parched land where silence reigns,
Beauty grows amidst the pains.
Celestial whispers breathe in life,
Turning strife into sweetest light.

Ethereal Glows in the Woodland Haze

In the hush of the misty morn,
Ethereal glows, the day is born.
Whispers twirl among the trees,
Dancing lightly with the breeze.

Flickering lights, like fairy dust,
Fill the air with magic's trust.
Shadows play where sunlight weaves,
In this land where life believes.

Misty trails entwine the roots,
Where laughter sings in hidden shoots.
Each step a note in nature's song,
Guiding souls where they belong.

Mirthful spirits greet the day,
As woodland dreams drift and sway.
Among the ferns and soft green beds,
Ethereal magic gently spreads.

Cascading light through leaves cascades,
In this realm where hope cascades.
Woodland hues, a painter's muse,
In every heart, the light ensues.

Mystical Radiance of the Twilight Glade

In the twilight's gentle haze,
Whispers weave through ancient trees,
Glimmers dance on leaves ablaze,
Magic sways upon the breeze.

Flickering lights like fireflies,
Chanting secrets, softly near,
As the moon begins to rise,
Casting dreams that disappear.

Echoes murmur, soft and low,
In this realm of twilight's grace,
Where the shadows lightly flow,
And the stars find their place.

Petals lift in silken night,
Bathed in silver, pure, and bright,
Nature sings a soothing tune,
Cradled in the arms of June.

Fables spun in light's embrace,
Guarded whispers in the glade,
In this haven, time and space,
Blend in dreams that never fade.

Secrets of the Sun-Drenched Glade

In the dawn where daylight spills,
Golden rays on emerald floor,
Bees hum sweetly, nature fills,
Every heart with tales of yore.

Leaves whisper in the morning air,
Dancing lightly in the sun,
Secrets shared with gentle care,
Join the chorus, every one.

Berries glisten, ripe and sweet,
Color bursts, alive and bold,
Every path, a treat to greet,
Stories waiting to be told.

Sun-kissed flowers start to sway,
With the breeze, a joyous sigh,
In the glade, where shadows play,
Life's enchantments flutter by.

Underneath the sky so wide,
Nature's canvas, bright and new,
In this realm where dreams abide,
Magic lingers, pure and true.

Luminance Lurking in the Thicket

In the thicket, shadows blend,
Flickers of a hidden light,
Secrets twine and spirits mend,
Veils of dusk begin to bite.

Branches arch, an emerald crown,
Softly hushed, the world unfolds,
Glimmers twirl but never drown,
Tales of magic yet untold.

A wise owl blinks through the dark,
Casting wisdom, ancient, deep,
In this wild, enchanting park,
Where the echoes dare to leap.

Moonlight drapes its silver thread,
Over thorns and tangled vines,
In this quiet place, we're led,
To remember what divine.

Every breath, a moment's grace,
Luminance in every sigh,
In the thicket, find your place,
Where the heart learns how to fly.

Chasing Shadows Under Celestial Boughs

Under boughs, so wide and deep,
Where the shadows softly creep,
Waves of twilight start to weave,
In the night, what dreams conceive.

Stars peek through the foliage green,
Casting glimmers on the ground,
Whispers float where none have been,
In this silence, magic's found.

Figures dance in dreams untold,
Chasing light and woven threads,
Stories from the nights of old,
Guide us softly where hope spreads.

With each step, the world does sigh,
In the glades where shadows play,
Hearts awakened, souls fly high,
Celebrating the end of day.

Beneath the stars, we find our way,
Chasing shadows, lost in flight,
In this realm where dreams hold sway,
And the past glimmers in light.

Twilight Serenades of the Nomad's Heart

In the dusk, where shadows meet,
Whispers weave a soft retreat.
A nomad's heart, so wild and free,
Seeks the twilight, where dreams may be.

Stars awaken, one by one,
Painting stories begun in fun.
The breeze carries tales untold,
Of adventures brave and bold.

A distant howl, a call to roam,
The desert sings, it feels like home.
Each winding path, a songbird flies,
Underneath vast, enchanted skies.

Footprints left, in sands of gold,
Echoes of the journeys bold.
The night unveils a canvas bright,
In the arms of gentle night.

In solitude, the heart does dance,
Embraced by fate, a fleeting chance.
The stars pour secrets, soft and sweet,
In this twilight, life feels complete.

Stars Among the Cactus Blooms

Beneath the moon, the blooms ignite,
Cacti stand, a splendid sight.
Dancing lights, the stars align,
Whispering secrets, divine design.

Every thorn, a story shared,
Of desert nights, where hearts have dared.
Silent vows beneath the glow,
Planting seeds of love to grow.

A breeze carries laughter, soft and light,
Guiding souls through the peaceful night.
Stars watch over, bright and true,
Painting dreams in every hue.

Among the blooms, the shadows play,
Remarkable beauty, night and day.
In this garden, life takes flight,
Underneath the starry light.

As dawn approaches, colors blend,
The cactus blooms, an endless friend.
Each petal holds a wish, a bliss,
A moment caught in timeless kiss.

Radiant Enigmas of the Desert Hearth

In flickering flames, stories rise,
The hearth exhales, in whispered sighs.
Mysteries dwell, warm and bright,
Embers glow, revealing night.

Every stone, a witness old,
To laughter shared and hearts consoled.
The desert air, so rich and deep,
Holds secrets the stillness keeps.

A dance of shadows, wild and free,
Echoes of our history.
The moon casts spells, both fierce and kind,
Leaving heartbeats well-defined.

The fragrant sagebrush swirling near,
Wraps us close, dispels our fear.
Each moment waltzes through the dark,
The hearth's embrace, a tender spark.

From the night's depths, a promise glows,
Through radiant enigmas, love bestows.
In the silence, listen close,
To the heart's truth, a haunting prose.

Shimmering Tales of the Sunken Glades

In hidden valleys, whispers flow,
Where secret waters shimmer low.
Sunken glades, a world apart,
Tales of magic ever start.

Rippling streams hold stories vast,
Of time forgotten, shadows cast.
Each glimmer speaks of days gone by,
Where echoes linger, never shy.

With ferns that dance and flowers bright,
The glades awaken to the night.
Stars settle gently on emerald leaves,
Where fantasy forever weaves.

Beneath the surface, dreams reside,
In shimmering currents, worlds abide.
Each breath of wind, a lover's sigh,
Beneath the clouds, where spirits fly.

In these tales, forever dwell,
Life's sweet sorrows, love's soft spell.
In hidden beauty, we find grace,
In the sunken glades, a warm embrace.

Spirits of the Saguaro's Shade

In the dusk where shadows sway,
Spirits whisper, lost and gray.
Beneath the arms of cactus tall,
Echoes linger, beckoning call.

Time moves slow in this sacred land,
Footsteps trace where silence stands.
In gentle winds, their tales unfold,
Secrets of the days of old.

Stars emerge as night descends,
With every breeze, the magic bends.
In the saguaro's binding clasp,
Timeless wonders we still grasp.

Nature's pulse, a steady thrum,
In the quiet, whispers hum.
The spirits watch, their presence clear,
Inviting hearts to draw near.

So linger long, and listen well,
In the shade, where stories dwell.
A world alive in each soft sigh,
Within this realm, dreams never die.

Mirage of the Elven Hollow

Deep within the forest glades,
An elven hollow softly fades.
With shimmering light, the pathways gleam,
A whisper of an ancient dream.

Elven laughter floats on air,
Dancing leaves, a magic rare.
In every shadow, secrets hide,
While enchanted creatures bide.

A silver stream flows bright and clear,
Drawing wanderers ever near.
Its gentle murmur sings in tune,
With the melody of the moon.

Wrought from stars and earth below,
In twilight hues, their wonders flow.
Mirage of dreams beneath the boughs,
In elven whispers, fate allows.

So tread with care, and hold your breath,
For in this hollow lies sweet death.
In the magic of the night,
Chase the mirage, find the light.

Flickers in the Twilight Tangle

In the forest where shadows play,
Flickers dance at end of day.
Ghostly lights weave through the trees,
A tapestry of whispered pleas.

Underneath the canopy thick,
Glimmers pulse like a heart's tick.
Curious souls will chase the glow,
In the twilight, where secrets flow.

Branches reach like fingers wide,
Holding tales that must confide.
In the dusk, a magic new,
Yearning hearts embrace the hue.

The air is thick with wonder's feel,
Every flicker, a chance to heal.
In the tangle of the night,
We find solace, we find light.

So venture forth, in shadows roam,
The twilight calls you to your home.
As fireflies weave their dreamy song,
In flickering paths, you belong.

Phantom Lights in the Desert Night

Beneath the vast cerulean dome,
Phantom lights make the desert home.
They shimmer soft on sands so gold,
Tales of wanderers faintly told.

As moonlight spills on cactus tall,
Shadows stretch, like spirits call.
In the silence, whispers blend,
Every moment, time to spend.

Mirages flicker in the heat,
An enticing dance, a heart's repeat.
With every glint, the stories flow,
From vanished lands where legends grow.

The desert's breath is wild and free,
Buffeted by an unseen plea.
Through spectral lights, mysteries ignite,
Veils of shadows in the night.

So wander where the phantoms drift,
In their glow, your spirit shift.
With each step and each heartbeat's thread,
In desert's night, find life instead.

Elven Radiance on Parched Soil

In hidden glades where sunlight glows,
Elven whispers softly bestow.
Among the roots, a blessing flows,
As ancient magic gently grows.

A silver mist on thirsty land,
Gathered dreams by nature's hand.
Life restored where shadows stand,
Together in this timeless span.

Beneath the trees with bark so bright,
They weave their tales in morning light.
Each sparkling drop, a tender sight,
Awakens hearts to pure delight.

With laughter ringing clear and true,
The forest dances, old yet new.
A promise bright in every hue,
Elven grace in all they do.

In parched soil where hope was lost,
A symphony without a cost.
Resilient dreams amid the frost,
This harmony, no soul can exhaust.

Dance of the Starlit Petals

When moonlight casts its silver net,
Petals twirl, a ballet set.
In twilight's breath, they softly fret,
A dance that none would dare forget.

The evening hums a gentle tune,
As flowers sway beneath the moon.
With every step, they seek to swoon,
In night's embrace, the world in bloom.

Each fragrant waltz, a tale to share,
In gardens bold, beyond compare.
With secrets spun in fragrant air,
They paint the night with faintest flair.

A twinkling star, a guide above,
As petals weave their tale of love.
A tapestry kissed by the dove,
In nature's dream, we find our grove.

So sway, dear petals, one more night,
In harmony, 'neath starlit light.
A melody that feels just right,
In timeless dance, hearts take flight.

Illumination in the Whispering Winds

The whispering winds call forth the dawn,
As secrets of the night are drawn.
They carry stories, soft and fawn,
On breezes woven, old yet spawn.

Through swaying trees their voices weave,
A gentle breath we dare believe.
In every sigh, the dreams conceive,
A warmth amidst the cool reprieve.

Illuminated by the sun's embrace,
Each shadow dances, finds its place.
The world alive, a fleeting grace,
In every gust, a soft embrace.

The foliage whispers, gleams, and sways,
In harmony that ever plays.
Among the branches, light displays,
A tapestry of golden rays.

So listen close to nature's song,
In every breath where we belong.
The winds remind us, we are strong,
Illuminated, life moves along.

Phosphorescent Dreams of the Reckless Oasis

Beneath the stars in deserts vast,
An oasis blooms, a dream amassed.
With phosphorescent colors cast,
A hidden world, enchanted, fast.

In whispers soft, the waters gleam,
Reflecting every fleeting dream.
In moonlit nights where shadows teem,
The heart ignites with each new scheme.

Amidst the sands, lost souls will find,
A refuge sweet, a path unlined.
Where hopes converge, and hearts unwind,
In reckless joy, our fates aligned.

A symphony of light appears,
As laughter echoes through the years.
In phosphorescent pools like tears,
We dive into the depth of fears.

So come, dear wanderers, embrace the night,
In reckless dreams, we take our flight.
An oasis blooms, a pure delight,
With phosphorescent magic bright.

Nighttime Echoing of the Dune Spirits

In the cool embrace of midnight air,
Dunes whisper secrets, wild and rare.
Spirits dance in shadows, soft and light,
Echoing laughter in the heart of night.

Silver sands shimmer under the pale moon,
Carried by winds that softly croon.
Footprints vanish, lost to time's own hand,
As dreams awaken in this timeless land.

Stars like lanterns, bright in the sky,
Guide the lost travelers who wander by.
Each grain holds stories, tales untold,
Of ancient spirits, daring and bold.

A lullaby murmurs through the chill air,
Ancient voices that weave a snare.
In twilight's embrace, all fears take flight,
Under the gaze of the watchful night.

So if you hear the desert's sweet song,
Know that the spirits in the night belong.
With every echo, a tale to convey,
In the realm where the dunes softly sway.

Luminous Realms Beneath the Wanderer's Moon

Beneath the moon's watchful, gentle glow,
Lies a world where soft wonders flow.
Whispers of magic fill the night air,
Luminous realms that dance without care.

Trees stand tall, their shadows entwined,
Echoing stories of hearts redesign.
Beneath their boughs, secrets are shared,
With every flicker, enchantments declared.

The brook sparkles with light's gentle dance,
Inviting all wanderers with chance.
Elusive beings weave in and out,
In a tapestry woven of joy and doubt.

Crickets perform in a chorus of sound,
Their rhythm the heartbeat of dreams profound.
A symphony plays in the moon's silver light,
Guiding each traveler into the night.

So linger a while in this magical place,
Feel the embrace of the moon's soft face.
For in the realms where dreams take flight,
The wanderer's heart finds pure delight.

Tales of the Arcane Glow

In a world where shadows meet the light,
Tales unfold in the still of night.
Whispers of magic linger and spin,
In the arcane glow, adventures begin.

Books of old are dusted and read,
Stories awaken, both living and dead.
Echoes of wizards weave through the text,
In spells and chants, the future's perplexed.

A flicker of fire in the hearth so bright,
Illuminates faces in the soft twilight.
Countless creatures from lore come to play,
In this charmed realm where dreams sway.

With each turn of page, a new path revealed,
Mysteries waiting to be unsealed.
In the glow of the arcane, secrets unfurl,
Binding the hearts of this enchanting world.

So gather around, dear friends, take heed,
In the stories we share, a magic seed.
For within every tale, a spark lies in tow,
In the wonderment found in the arcane glow.

Emissaries of the Sylvan Night

In woods untouched by the passing time,
Where silence sings in a haunting rhyme.
Emissaries glide on wings of grace,
Guardians of secrets, embracing the space.

The trees are alive with whispers untold,
Branches cradling the stars, bright and bold.
Fae and spirits dance in the gleam,
Weaving through shadows, lost in a dream.

Moss carpets the ground, a soft, green sea,
Where each step carries a hint of mystery.
Moonlight filters through leaves overhead,
As stories echo where the brave dare tread.

Hushed are the creatures, the night their domain,
Awakening hearts to the wonders of rain.
With every rustle, enchantments take flight,
In the realm of the sylvan, alive with light.

So venture forth, take a breath of the night,
For the emissaries dwell just out of sight.
In a world of magic, where old ways remain,
The essence of nature shall always sustain.

Ephemeral Glows of Dusk's Retreat

In the quiet of dusk, the shadows play,
Colors dance gently, then fade away.
Stars shimmer softly, in velvet skies,
Hopes take flight on the wings of sighs.

Leaves whisper secrets, the night draws near,
Echoes of laughter, both far and near.
A world painted gold in a fleeting chance,
As night weaves its magic, we twirl and dance.

Dreams stretch like shadows beneath the trees,
Carried on currents of soft, sighing breeze.
Crickets sing lullabies, sweet and low,
As flickers of light in the dark start to glow.

Time wanders softly, it ebbs and flows,
Moments like petals, each fragile rose.
A twilight embrace, warm and divine,
In the ephemeral glow, our spirits align.

Horizon Chasers in Dreamy Landscapes

Across the horizon, where magic unfolds,
We chase after dreams that the sunset holds.
Mountains like giants, rise up in the mist,
Each valley a whisper, too sweet to resist.

With hearts wide open, we venture afar,
Guided by starlight and the light of a star.
Fields of wildflowers sway gently in dreams,
Painting the landscape in vibrant sunbeams.

With whispers of hope tucked beneath every tree,
We gather the wonders that set our hearts free.
In every encounter, a story takes flight,
A tapestry woven in day and in night.

We dance with the shadows, we sing with the dawn,
Embracing the moments before they are gone.
In places uncharted, where spirits entwine,
We follow the whispers, our destinies shine.

Reveries of the Soft Sand Winds

On shores softly kissed by the golden sun,
The tides weave a tale, where dreams are spun.
Waves cradle secrets, the sea's gentle breath,
Carrying whispers of life and of death.

Footprints like stories trace paths in the sand,
Each grain holds a memory, a touch of the hand.
Seagulls cry out, their wings broad and free,
A dance with the currents, a wild jubilee.

In the caress of the wind, we find our way,
Guided by whispers that time can't betray.
Each moment, a treasure, each sigh, a refrain,
Reveries shimmer like bright silver rain.

As twilight descends, colors blush and fade,
Promises linger, like dreams unmade.
In the hush of the evening, our hopes take flight,
With soft sand beneath us, we dream through the night.

Twilight Whispers in Elder Trees

In the heart of the forest, where the wild things roam,
Elder trees stand proud, their branches a home.
Twilight whispers secrets, in rustling leaves,
Stories of ages, the wind softly weaves.

Moss carpets the ground, a soft, emerald hue,
As shadows stretch long in the fading view.
Birdsong lingers, like echoes of light,
Kissed by the magic of coming night.

Crickets in chorus, a symphony's rise,
Filling the silence with their serenades.
In the twilight's embrace, the world seems to pause,
A moment of wonder, a magical cause.

With every rustle, the night comes alive,
In flickers of fireflies, where dreams can thrive.
Amongst elder trees, our spirits find peace,
In whispers of twilight, our worries release.

As stars twinkle bright, in the starlit expanse,
We find our way forward, in time's gentle dance.
So let us wander, where magic unveils,
In the twilight whispers, where wonder prevails.

Veil of Light in Hidden Hollows

In the whisper of the leaves, they dance,
Glimmers lost in twilight's trance.
Moonbeams spill on mossy stone,
Calling spirits, all alone.

A gentle breeze awakens dreams,
As silver starlight softly gleams.
Each shadow shimmers, secrets weave,
In hidden hollows, hearts believe.

With laughter faint, the fairies play,
In echoes of the end of day.
A tranquil hush embraces all,
As twilight's magic starts to call.

Whispers threaded in the night,
Guide the weary with their light.
Each hidden path, a story told,
Of wonders young and echoes old.

So tread softly, kindred souls,
Among the hollows, where time rolls.
For in the veil of light so bright,
Lies the heart of endless night.

Serenade of the Night-Blooming Flora

In twilight's hand, the petals spread,
A symphony where whispers wed.
Night-blooming flowers softly sigh,
As dreams unfold beneath the sky.

Their colors dance in fragrant air,
Awakening the moon's soft stare.
Each blossom knows the lover's tune,
As shadows stretch beneath the moon.

Crickets play a lullaby sweet,
While starlit paths entwine their beat.
In twilight's arms, they sway and twine,
In harmony, a world divine.

The gentle sighs of petals bloom,
Cast away the lingering gloom.
A serenade of soft delight,
Draped in mystique of the night.

So let us pause, and breathe it in,
Where every stem is drawn to spin.
In the garden, secrets flow,
In night's embrace, we come to grow.

Silhouettes of Sylvan Guardians

Among the trees, the shadows rise,
Silhouettes beneath the skies.
Rustling leaves in whispered grace,
Guardians of this ancient place.

Their forms like smoke in twilight drift,
A timeless dance, the forest's gift.
Echoes of an age long past,
Where silence holds the die is cast.

With every rustle, tales unfold,
Of secret dreams and hearts that are bold.
Beneath the boughs where shadows play,
The sylvan guardians find their way.

In glades of gold, their spirits dwell,
Echoing the forest's spell.
Eyes like embers, flickers bright,
Guide lost souls through the night.

So wander near, and heed the call,
Of ancient truths within the thrall.
For in their watchful gaze, you'll find,
The wealth of time, the ties that bind.

Secrets of the Twilight Grove

In twilight's hush, the secrets wait,
Nestled deep, beyond the gate.
Whispers linger, soft and sweet,
In the grove where shadows meet.

Every branch a story holds,
Of magic spun and light enfolds.
Lost paths twist where no one goes,
In every heart, a longing grows.

The rustle of leaves, a soft refrain,
Sings of joy, and dances of pain.
Twilight cloaks the world so wide,
Where countless dreams and fears reside.

On mossy beds of emerald hue,
The secrets bloom, their tales renew.
As twilight sways, the night ignites,
With every star, a wish ignites.

In hidden shades, the truth will gleam,
Within the dark, the light will beam.
So tread with care, as shadows move,
In the twilight grove, the heart will prove.

Radiance in the Swaying Dunes

Beneath the moon's soft glow,
The dunes whisper secrets low.
Stars blend with sands so fine,
In the night, their light does shine.

Footprints dance in twilight's hue,
Tracing paths both old and new.
Eager winds carry tales of old,
As dreams in silken threads unfold.

Shadows play where shadows meet,
A tale of wonder, bittersweet.
Echoes of a distant song,
In this realm, we all belong.

Sandcastles of our hearts arise,
Underneath the vast, dark skies.
Each grain a wish, a fleeting chance,
In the moonlight's tender dance.

When dawn breaks to kiss the land,
The magic fades like grains of sand.
Yet in our hearts, the stories stay,
A radiant truth in light's soft sway.

Fable of the Dusk's Embrace

In the hush of the fading light,
Stars emerge, twinkling bright.
The sky blushes with shades of gold,
A tale of dusk quietly told.

Whispers of the night begin,
Caressing where the day has been.
Creatures stir beneath the trees,
As if they dance on the evening breeze.

Moonlight weaves through branches bare,
Casting dreams with utmost care.
Every shadow tells a tale,
Of adventures both grand and frail.

Lost in the fable's sweet delight,
Hearts drift softly into night.
Hand in hand, we softly roam,
In dusk's embrace, we find our home.

As the stars weave their silver thread,
We collect stories that must be read.
In this gentle, magic hour,
We bloom like words, each like a flower.

Glinting Treasures of the Nightscape

In the velvet of the night,
Stars fall like jewels, bright and light.
Oceans whisper secrets deep,
As the world melts into sleep.

Diamonds dance on silver streams,
Chasing shadows, weaving dreams.
A tapestry of luminous grace,
Each glimmer holds a soft embrace.

Night blooms with a fragrant song,
Where hopes and wishes both belong.
The universe, vast and clear,
Wraps our hearts with starlit cheer.

In the glow of a lantern's gleam,
We gather beneath twilight's beam.
Each treasure held, a story spun,
As the nightscape reveals its fun.

With every twinkle, every spark,
We find joy within the dark.
In each treasure that we see,
Lies the magic of you and me.

Undercurrents of Light in the Night Desert

In the desert's silent sigh,
Stars unfold like dreams on high.
The moon, a guide in endless space,
Illuminates each hidden trace.

Whispers of the cool night air,
Lead us to places rare and fair.
Footsteps soft on shifting sand,
In this vast, enchanted land.

The light dances on the crest,
Of dunes where secrets lay to rest.
Each shadow casts a fleeting thought,
Of treasures found and battles fought.

As constellations weave their lore,
We wander through the night's sweet door.
In this land where silence reigns,
The heart knows joy, yet feels the pains.

With every moment, we ignite,
The undercurrents of pure light.
In the night desert, dreams arise,
Reflecting hope beneath our skies.

www.ingramcontent.com/pod-product-compliance
Ingram Content Group UK Ltd.
Pitfield, Milton Keynes, MK11 3LW, UK
UKHW021514280125
4335UKWH00036B/852